# ROSE

# ROSE

poems by Li-Young Lee

foreword by Gerald Stern

**BOA Editions, Ltd. • Rochester, New York**

Some of the poems herein previously appeared in the following publications: *The American Poetry Review:* "Early in the Morning," "Persimmons," "Water," "Dreaming of Hair," "The Gift," "My Indigo," "My Sleeping Loved Ones;" *The Brockport Review:* "Braiding;" *Iowa Review:* "Eating Together;" *Madison Review:* "Irises," "Falling: The Code;" *Missouri State Review:* "Rain Diary," "Eating Alone;" *The Pushcart Prize VIII:* "Persimmons" (reprint); *The Pushcart Prize IX:* "The Gift" (reprint); *The Pushcart Prize XI:* "Eating Together" (reprint).

I would like to mention my indebtedness to my family and my gratitude to the following persons: Bill Heyen, Peter Marchant, Ed Ochester, Tony Piccione, Al Poulin, Mike Servoss, Gerald Stern.

I am grateful to The Commonwealth of Pennsylvania and the Pennsylvania Council on the Arts, and the Illinois Arts Council for grants which aided in the completion of this book.

—L-Y. L.

BOA Editions, Ltd., 260 East Avenue, Rochester, NY 14420.

ISBN: 0-918526-53-1

99 98 97          14 13 12

Publications by BOA Editions, Ltd., a not-for-profit corporation under section 501(c)(3) of the United States Internal Revenue Service Code, are made possible in part with the assistance of grants from the Literature Program of the New York State Council on the Arts and the Literature Program of the National Endowment for the Arts, a Federal Agency.

BOA logo by Mirko.
Cover design: Li-Lin Lee
Designed and typeset at Visual Studies Workshop, Rochester, N.Y.

BOA Editions, Ltd.
Alexandra Northrop, Chair
A. Poulin, Jr., Founder and President (1976-1996)
260 East Avenue
Rochester, NY 14604

*For Donna*

# CONTENTS

# FOREWORD

When I first came across Li-Young Lee's poetry I was amazed by the large vision, the deep seriousness and the almost heroic ideal, reminiscent more of John Keats, Rainer Maria Rilke and perhaps Theodore Roethke than William Carlos Williams on the one hand or T.S. Eliot on the other. He was an undergraduate student at the University of Pittsburgh at that time—I think it was 1978 or 79—and I was teaching a workshop in the graduate school, which I allowed him to sign up for. I remember that, with the exception of Lee, the students were writing a fairly low-keyed poem based on specific "domestic" experiences where the "value" of the poem consisted of persuading the reader of the truth—and significance—of the experience. It was fourth, or third, or fifth generation W.C.W. I don't think Li-Young Lee's choice to move in the direction of Rilke *et al.* was based on ignorance of the dominant mode; he was responding to an urge which has nothing or little to do with such political matters. Nor am I saying that he has bypassed or ignored Williams. Rather he has used him in his own way. Indeed there are a number of Lee's poems—"Dreaming of Hair" for instance—which show a direct link to the later Williams, that glorious theory-defying Williams of the last period.

What characterizes Lee's poetry is a certain humility, a kind of cunning, a love of plain speech, a search for wisdom and understanding—but more like a sad than a desperate search—a willingness to let the sublime enter his field of concentration and take over, a devotion to language, a belief in its holiness, a pursuit of certain Chinese ideas, or Chinese memories, without any self-conscious ethnocentricity, and a moving personal search for redemption, which takes the form of understanding and coming to peace with a powerful, stubborn, remote, passionate and loving father. I think, in fact, that understanding, even accepting, the father is the critical event, the critical "myth" in Lee's poetry.

This is not a quaint and literary father-figure he is writing and thinking about. It is a real father, an extraordinary and heroic figure—at least as Lee sees him: personal physician to Mao, medical advisor to Sukarno, political prisoner in an Indonesian swamp and, finally, Presbyterian minister in a tiny western Pennsylvania town, full of rage and mystery and pity, blind and silent at the end. What makes him work as a mythical figure in Lee's poems is that it is a real human being, however converted in Lee's mind, that Lee is searching for, and his search is personal, and essential, for him, the poet—the man. If the father does become mythical, it is partly because of his dramatic, even tragic, life, and it is partly because Lee touches powerful emotional psychic layers in his search. But it is mostly because he has found the language to release those layers. The "father" in contemporary poetry tends to be either a pathetic soul or a bungler or a sweet loser, overwhelmed by the demands of family and culture and workplace. At very best he is a small hero who died early or escaped west or found the bottle and whom the poet, in his or her poem, is forgiving. The father in Lee's poems is nothing like that. He is more godlike. And the poet's job becomes not to benignly or tenderly forgive him, but to withstand him and comprehend him, and variously love and fear him. Maybe Lee—as a poet—is lucky to have had the father he had and the culture he had. Maybe they combine in such a way as to make his own poetry possible. Even unique.

I have tried to discover the art in these poems, to see how one line moves into the next, how one stanza flows into another, how the energy—and tension—is maintained, why it works better in some poems than in others. He is a difficult poet to analyze. The technique is not only not transparent but there is a certain effortlessness about the writing that disguises the complexity of technique. There is a debt to Whitman, and one to Roethke. Also, I think, to Herbert and Traherne. Among contemporaries, James Wright, Galway Kinnell, and Philip Levine. I sometimes think that technique, particularly in such poets, consists in finding the language that releases—even awakens—feelings, and that the poem as art object is best served by addressing those very feelings, that is, the language of those feelings. This is not to say that technique takes care of itself. It is to reaffirm that art is mystery and our critical prose only begins to penetrate it.

There are poems of Li-Young Lee I return to over and over. I am amazed at their simplicity and their grace and their loveliness. I love "The Gift," "Dreaming of Hair," "Eating Alone." The art of the simple is full of peril. There is such a fine line between the converted and the unconverted. This is such risk. And I'm not sure anyone can explain why the poem sometimes works and sometimes doesn't. I find myself also admiring the shorter set pieces like "Irises" and "Early in the Morning" and reading with great delight his long poem, "Always a Rose," which only a poet of true forgetfulness and true vision would be able to bring off. This poem is almost different in kind from the others, partly because of its length, partly because of the disjunct but accumulative sections, and partly because of the concentration on the mystic symbol. The rose becomes not something to stare at, but to consume. The rose, which is history, the past, a "doomed profane flower" to be adored and destroyed. To be eaten. Like the speaker.

I celebrate Li-Young Lee's fine book of poems. I think we are in the presence of true spirit.

—Gerald Stern

**I.**

## EPISTLE

Of wisdom, splendid columns of light
waking sweet foreheads,
I know nothing

but what I've glimpsed in my most hopeful of daydreams.
Of a world without end,
amen,

I know nothing,
but what I sang of once with others,
all of us standing in the vaulted room.

But there is wisdom
in the hour in which a boy
sits in his room listening

to the sound of weeping
coming from some other room
of his father's house,

and that boy was me, and he
listened without understanding, and was soon frightened
by how the monotonous sobs resembled laughter.

All of this while noon became vast day,
while sunlight and the clock
gave birth to melancholy,

before the days grew vacant,
the sun grew terrible, the clock stopped,
and melancholy gave up to grief.

All of this
in a dead hour of a dead day,
among doors closed for nap or prayer.

Who was weeping? Why?
Did the boy fall asleep?
Did he flee that house? Is he there now?

Before it all gets wiped away, let me say,
there is wisdom in the slender hour
which arrives between two shadows.

It is not heavenly and it is not sweet.
It is accompanied by steady human weeping,
and twin furrows between the brows,

but it is what I know,
and so am able to tell.

## THE GIFT

To pull the metal splinter from my palm
my father recited a story in a low voice.
I watched his lovely face and not the blade.
Before the story ended, he'd removed
the iron sliver I thought I'd die from.

I can't remember the tale,
but hear his voice still, a well
of dark water, a prayer.
And I recall his hands,
two measures of tenderness
he laid against my face,
the flames of discipline
he raised above my head.

Had you entered that afternoon
you would have thought you saw a man
planting something in a boy's palm,
a silver tear, a tiny flame.
Had you followed that boy
you would have arrived here,
where I bend over my wife's right hand.

Look how I shave her thumbnail down
so carefully she feels no pain.
Watch as I lift the splinter out.
I was seven when my father
took my hand like this,

and I did not hold that shard
between my fingers and think,
*Metal that will bury me,*
christen it Little Assassin,
Ore Going Deep for My Heart.
And I did not lift up my wound and cry,
*Death visited here!*
I did what a child does
when he's given something to keep.
I kissed my father.

# PERSIMMONS

In sixth grade Mrs. Walker
slapped the back of my head
and made me stand in the corner
for not knowing the difference
between *persimmon* and *precision*.
How to choose

persimmons. This is precision.
Ripe ones are soft and brown-spotted.
Sniff the bottoms. The sweet one
will be fragrant. How to eat:
put the knife away, lay down newspaper.
Peel the skin tenderly, not to tear the meat.
Chew the skin, suck it,
and swallow. Now, eat
the meat of the fruit,
so sweet,
all of it, to the heart.

Donna undresses, her stomach is white.
In the yard, dewy and shivering
with crickets, we lie naked,
face-up, face-down.
I teach her Chinese.
Crickets:    *chiu chiu.* Dew:    I've forgotten.
Naked:    I've forgotten.
*Ni, wo*:    you and me.
I part her legs,
remember to tell her
she is beautiful as the moon.

Other words
that got me into trouble were
*fight* and *fright, wren* and *yarn.*
Fight was what I did when I was frightened,
fright was what I felt when I was fighting.

Wrens are small, plain birds,
yarn is what one knits with.
Wrens are soft as yarn.
My mother made birds out of yarn.
I loved to watch her tie the stuff;
a bird, a rabbit, a wee man.

Mrs. Walker brought a persimmon to class
and cut it up
so everyone could taste
a *Chinese apple*. Knowing
it wasn't ripe or sweet, I didn't eat
but watched the other faces.

My mother said every persimmon has a sun
inside, something golden, glowing,
warm as my face.

Once, in the cellar, I found two wrapped in newspaper,
forgotten and not yet ripe.
I took them and set both on my bedroom windowsill,
where each morning a cardinal
sang, *The sun, the sun.*

Finally understanding
he was going blind,
my father sat up all one night
waiting for a song, a ghost.
I gave him the persimmons,
swelled, heavy as sadness,
and sweet as love.

This year, in the muddy lighting
of my parents' cellar, I rummage, looking
for something I lost.
My father sits on the tired, wooden stairs,
black cane between his knees,
hand over hand, gripping the handle.

He's so happy that I've come home.
I ask how his eyes are, a stupid question.
*All gone*, he answers.

Under some blankets, I find a box.
Inside the box I find three scrolls.
I sit beside him and untie
three paintings by my father:
Hibiscus leaf and a white flower.
Two cats preening.
Two persimmons, so full they want to drop from the cloth.

He raises both hands to touch the cloth,
asks, *Which is this?*

*This is persimmons, Father.*

*Oh, the feel of the wolftail on the silk,*
*the strength, the tense*
*precision in the wrist.*
*I painted them hundreds of times*
*eyes closed. These I painted blind.*
*Some things never leave a person:*
*scent of the hair of one you love,*
*the texture of persimmons,*
*in your palm, the ripe weight.*

## THE WEIGHT OF SWEETNESS

No easy thing to bear, the weight of sweetness.

Song, wisdom, sadness, joy: sweetness
equals three of any of these gravities.

See a peach bend
the branch and strain the stem until
it snaps.
Hold the peach, try the weight, sweetness
and death so round and snug
in your palm.
And, so, there is
the weight of memory:

Windblown, a rain-soaked
bough shakes, showering
the man and the boy.
They shiver in delight,
and the father lifts from his son's cheek
one green leaf
fallen like a kiss.

The good boy hugs a bag of peaches
his father has entrusted
to him.
Now he follows
his father, who carries a bagful in each arm.
See the look on the boy's face
as his father moves
faster and farther ahead, while his own steps
flag, and his arms grow weak, as he labors
under the weight
of peaches.

## FROM BLOSSOMS

From blossoms comes
this brown paper bag of peaches
we bought from the boy
at the bend in the road where we turned toward
signs painted *Peaches.*

From laden boughs, from hands,
from sweet fellowship in the bins,
comes nectar at the roadside, succulent
peaches we devour, dusty skin and all,
comes the familiar dust of summer, dust we eat.

O, to take what we love inside,
to carry within us an orchard, to eat
not only the skin, but the shade,
not only the sugar, but the days, to hold
the fruit in our hands, adore it, then bite into
the round jubilance of peach.

There are days we live
as if death were nowhere
in the background; from joy
to joy to joy, from wing to wing,
from blossom to blossom to
impossible blossom, to sweet impossible blossom.

## DREAMING OF HAIR

Ivy ties the cellar door
in autumn, in summer morning glory
wraps the ribs of a mouse.
Love binds me to the one
whose hair I've found in my mouth,
whose sleeping head I kiss,
wondering is it death?
beauty?    this dark
star spreading in every direction from the crown of her head.

My love's hair is autumn hair, there
the sun ripens.
My fingers harvest the dark
vegetable of her body.
In the morning I remove it
from my tongue and
sleep again.

Hair spills
through my dream, sprouts
from my stomach, thickens my heart,
and tangles the brain. Hair ties the tongue dumb.
Hair ascends the tree
of my childhood—the willow
I climbed
one bare foot and hand at a time,
feeling the knuckles of the gnarled tree, hearing
my father plead from his window, *Don't fall!*

In my dream I fly
past summers and moths,
to the thistle
caught in my mother's hair, the purple one
I touched and bled for,

to myself at three, sleeping
beside her, waking with her hair in my mouth.

Along a slippery twine of her black hair
my mother ties *ko-tze* knots for me:
fish and lion heads, chrysanthemum buds, the heads
of Chinamen, black-haired and frowning.

Li-En, my brother, frowns when he sleeps.
I push back his hair, stroke his brow.
His hairline is our father's, three peaks pointing down.

What sprouts from the body
and touches the body?
What filters sunlight
and drinks moonlight?
Where have I misplaced my heart?
What stops wheels and great machines?
What tangles in the bough
and snaps the loom?

Out of the grave
my father's hair
bursts. A strand
pierces my left sole, shoots
up bone, past ribs,
to the broken heart it stitches,
then down,
swirling in the stomach, in the groin, and down,
through the right foot.

What binds me to this earth?
What remembers the dead
and grows toward them?

I'm tired of thinking.
I long to taste the world with a kiss.

I long to fly into hair with kisses and weeping,
remembering an afternoon
when, kissing my sleeping father, I saw for the first time
behind the thick swirl of his black hair,
the mole of wisdom,
a lone planet spinning slowly.

Sometimes my love is melancholy
and I hold her head in my hands.
Sometimes I recall our hair grows after death.
Then, I must grab handfuls
of her hair, and, I tell you, there
are apples, walnuts, ships sailing, ships docking, and men
taking off their boots, their hearts breaking,
not knowing
which they love more, the water, or
their women's hair, sprouting from the head, rushing toward
    the feet.

## EARLY IN THE MORNING

While the long grain is softening
in the water, gurgling
over a low stove flame, before
the salted Winter Vegetable is sliced
for breakfast, before the birds,
my mother glides an ivory comb
through her hair, heavy
and black as calligrapher's ink.

She sits at the foot of the bed.
My father watches, listens for
the music of comb
against hair.

My mother combs,
pulls her hair back
tight, rolls it
around two fingers, pins it
in a bun to the back of her head.
For half a hundred years she has done this.
My father likes to see it like this.
He says it is kempt.

But I know
it is because of the way
my mother's hair falls
when he pulls the pins out.
Easily, like the curtains
when they untie them in the evening.

## WATER

The sound of 36 pines side by side surrounding
the yard and swaying all night like individual hymns is the sound
of water, which is the oldest sound,
the first sound we forgot.

At the ocean
my brother stands in water
to his knees, his chest bare, hard, his arms
thick and muscular. He is no swimmer.
In water
my sister is no longer
lonely. Her right leg is crooked and smaller
than her left, but she swims straight.
Her whole body is a glimmering fish.

Water is my father's life-sign.
Son of water who'll die by water,
the element which rules his life shall take it.
After being told so by a wise man in Shantung,
after almost drowning twice,
he avoided water. But the sign of water
is a flowing sign, going where its children go.

Water has invaded my father's
heart, swollen, heavy,
twice as large. Bloated
liver. Bloated legs.
The feet have become balloons.
A respirator mask makes him look
like a diver. When I lay my face
against his—the sound of water
returning.

The sound of washing
is the sound of sighing,

is the only sound
as I wash my father's feet—
those lonely twins
who have forgotten one another—
one by one in warm water
I tested with my wrist.
In soapy water
they're two dumb fish
whose eyes close in a filmy dream.

I dry, then powder them
with talc rising in clouds
like dust lifting
behind jeeps, a truck where he sat
bleeding through his socks.
1949, he's 30 years old,
his toenails pulled out,
his toes beaten a beautiful
violet that reminds him
of Hunan, barely morning
in the yard, and where
he walked, the grass springing back
damp and green.

The sound of rain
outlives us. I listen,
someone is whispering.
Tonight, it's water
the curtains resemble, water
drumming on the steel cellar door, water
we crossed to come to America,
water I'll cross to go back,
water which will kill my father.
The sac of water we live in.

## FALLING: THE CODE

1.

Through the night
the apples
outside my window
one by one let go
their branches and
drop to the lawn.
I can't see, but hear
the stem-snap, the plummet
through leaves, then
the final thump against the ground.

Sometimes two
at once, or one
right after another.
During long moments of silence
I wait
and wonder about the bruised bodies,
the terror of diving through air, and
think I'll go tomorrow
to find the newly fallen, but they
all look alike lying there
dewsoaked, disappearing before me.

2.
I lie beneath my window listening
to the sound of apples dropping in

the yard, a syncopated code I long to know,
which continues even as I sleep, and dream I know

the meaning of what I hear, each dull
thud of unseen apple-

body, the earth
falling to earth

once and forever, over
and over.

## NOCTURNE

That scraping of iron on iron when the wind
rises, what is it? Something the wind won't
quit with, but drags back and forth.
Sometimes faint, far, then suddenly, close, just
beyond the screened door, as if someone there
squats in the dark honing his wares against
my threshold. Half steel wire, half metal wing,
nothing and anything might make this noise
of saws and rasps, a creaking and groaning
of bone-growth, or body-death, marriages of rust,
or ore abraded. Tonight, something bows
that should not bend. Something stiffens that should
slide. Something, loose and not right,
rakes or forges itself all night.

## MY INDIGO

It's late. I've come
to find the flower which blossoms
like a saint dying upside down.
The rose won't do, nor the iris.
I've come to find the moody one, the shy one,
downcast, grave, and isolated.
Now, blackness gathers in the grass,
and I am on my hands and knees.
What is its name?

Little sister, my indigo,
my secret, vaginal and sweet,
you unfurl yourself shamelessly
toward the ground. You burn. You live
a while in two worlds
at once.

## IRISES

1.
In the night, in the wind, at the edge of the rain,
I find five irises, and call them lovely.
As if a woman, once, lay by them awhile,
then woke, rose, went, the memory of hair
lingers on their sweet tongues.

I'd like to tear these petals with my teeth.
I'd like to investigate these hairy selves,
their beauty and indifference. They hold
their breath all their lives
and open, open.

2.
We are not lovers, not brother and sister,
though we drift hand in hand through a hall
thrilling and burning as thought and desire
expire, and, over this dream of life,
this life of sleep, we waken dying—
violet becoming blue, growing
black, black—all that
an iris ever prays,
when it prays,
to be.

## EATING ALONE

I've pulled the last of the year's young onions.
The garden is bare now. The ground is cold,
brown and old. What is left of the day flames
in the maples at the corner of my
eye. I turn, a cardinal vanishes.
By the cellar door, I wash the onions,
then drink from the icy metal spigot.

Once, years back, I walked beside my father
among the windfall pears. I can't recall
our words. We may have strolled in silence. But
I still see him bend that way—left hand braced
on knee, creaky—to lift and hold to my
eye a rotten pear. In it, a hornet
spun crazily, glazed in slow, glistening juice.

It was my father I saw this morning
waving to me from the trees. I almost
called to him, until I came close enough
to see the shovel, leaning where I had
left it, in the flickering, deep green shade.

White rice steaming, almost done. Sweet green peas
fried in onions. Shrimp braised in sesame
oil and garlic. And my own loneliness.
What more could I, a young man, want.

## ALWAYS A ROSE

1.
What shape floats
in the dark window, what
ragged form?
Mouth, scream, edges
barbed, it balances
on a long, spiked, crooked
stem. I know now,
as if I'd never known, this
black shape within the night's black shape.

Dead daisies, shrivelled lilies, withered bodies
of dry chrysanthemums. Among these, and waste leaves
of yellow and brown fronds of palm and fern,
I came, and found
a rose
left for dead, heaped with the hopeless dead,
its petals still supple.
Of my brothers
one would have ignored it,
another ravished it, the third
would have pinned it to his chest and swaggered home.
My sister would rival its beauty,
my mother bow before it, then bear it
to my father's grave, where
he would grant it seven days,
then return and claim it forever.
I took it,
put it in water,
and set it on my windowsill.

2.

In the procession of summers and the arrivals of days
the roses marched by in a blur: the roses burning
in the coffin between my father's stiff hands.
The rose I mistook for blood on my sister's breast.
A red rose I thought was a mouth (it was mute),
a white rose I swore was my soul (it choked).
Black Chinese roses my grandmother
describes to anyone who'll listen;
the ones that tasted like grapes
when she ate them as a girl.
Terrible rose my brother inherited,
worm-eaten rose
of his brain, rose
of ruin in his poor life.
And it was roses that broke the back of the Book of Martyrs,
and roses my mother would touch and heal, but roses
which went on dying.

Always a rose,
in prayer and in fever,
in the sun and in the den.
Always that doomed, profane flower, that vertical flame
darkens my arrivals, announces my departures,
and sweetens my dying.
Always the blackening, the bruising, the late fragrance,
the opening to fullness and toward death.
Always a rose ready
to spill its petals, so that I must pluck
each of them, or crush
the whole thing in my fist.
Or I must cup it
in my hands, adore it,
in silence,
or, more often,
in words.

3.

When with arrows, night pierces you, rose,
I see most clearly
your true nature.
Small, auroral, your death is large.
You live, you die with me, in spite
of me, like my sleeping wife.
Lying here, with her at my right and you at my left,
the dying lies between the dying.

Bend closer, let me translate my nights and days.
Each finger is a brother or sister,
in each thumb is smudged the deaths I'm losing count of.
The left palm is the forsythia that never waved good-bye,
the right is my beloved pine dying from something no one knew.
My arms and legs are the rain in its opulence,
my face my mother's face.
My hair is also hers.
She inherited it from the horses
who recovered it from the night.
Here is what is left: a little brown, bits of black, a few specks
    of light.
Here are my shoulders and their winglessness,
my spine, the arc of love.
And here on my belly
is a stripe of skin, hairless
and the color of old blood.
Beginning at the navel, it descends into the tangled hairs.
Vestige, omen, this is the stain
which at my birth my father
traced with his finger
while pronouncing in dread
that I was born half girl.
So I was given the remedy of the rose,
made to eat you whole, swallow your medicinal taste.

Before the honey, before
the salty crystal,
I knew your bitterness,
a fresh shovel of dirt,
a bitterness rich with grief,
a black flavor far back in the throat,
one part soil, two parts root, and all the filaments of rain.
Question and answer in one
bud unfolding, you are what
the spade tastes with its sharp tongue,
what the earth utters in serious savors
more generous than salt, more memorable than sweetness,
something with a shadow the weight of a man
fallen asleep during incessant prayer,
a good, grave, exquisite
bitterness.

4.

Odorous and tender flower-
body, I eat you
to recall my first misfortune.
Little, bitter
body, I eat you
to understand my grave father.
Excellent body of layers tightly
wound around nothing,
I eat you to put my faith in grief.
Singed at the edges, dying
from the flame you live by, I
eat you to sink into
my own body. Secret body
of deep liquor,
I eat you
down to your secret.

5.

Listen now to something human.
I know moments measured
by a kiss, or a tear, a pass of the hand along a loved one's face.
I know lips that love me,
that return my kisses
by leaving on my cheek their salt.
And there is one I love, who hid her heart behind a stone.
Let there be a rose for her, who was poor,
who lived through ten bad years, and then ten more,
who took a lifetime to drain her bitter cup.
And there is one I love, smallest among us—
let there be a rose for him—
who was driven from the foreign schoolyards
by fists and yelling, who trembled in anger in each re-telling,
who played alone all the days,
though the afternoon trees were full of children.
And there is one I love who limps over this planet,
dragging her steel hip.
Always a rose for her.
And always a rose for one I love, lost
in another country, from whom I get year-old letters.
And always a rose for one I love
exiled from one republic and daily defeated in another,
who was shunned by brothers and stunned by God,
who couldn't sleep because of voices,
who raised his voice, then his hand
against his children, against his children
going. For him a rose, my lover of roses and of God,
who taught me to love the rose, and fed me roses, under whose windows
I planted roses, for whose tables I harvested roses,
who put his hand on my crown and purified me
in the name of the Father, of the Son, and of the Holy Ghost,

who said, *Get out! You're no longer my son!*
who never said, *Forgive me. Why do I die? Hold me, hold me.*
My father the Godly, he was the chosen.
My father almighty, full of good fear.
My father exhausted, my beloved.
My father among the roses and thorns.
My father rose, my father thorn.

6.

Not for the golden pears, rotten on the ground —
their sweetness their secret — not for the scent
of their dying did I go back to my father's house. Not for the grass
grown wild as his beard in his last months,
nor for the hard, little apples that littered the yard,
and vines, rampant on the porch, tying the door shut,
did I stand there, late, rain arriving.
The rain came. And where there is rain
there is time, and memory, and sometimes sweetness.
Where there is a son there is a father.
And if there is love there is
no forgetting, but regret rending
two shaggy hearts.
I said good-bye to the forsythia, flowerless for years.
I turned from the hive-laden pine.
Then, I saw it — you, actually.
Past the choked rhododendrons,
behind the perishing gladiolas, there
in the far corner of the yard, you, my rose,
lovely for nothing, lonely for no one,
stunning the afternoon
with your single flower ablaze.
I left that place, I let the rain
meditate on the brilliance of one blossom
quivering in the beginning downpour.

7.

Why do you stay away from me?
At what far edge
do you linger, trembler,
that you can't hear me call?
What is this liturgy, this
invocation, and to whom?
What are you to me? I'd tear you with my teeth!
Speak, speaking-flower!
Open me, thorn-flower!
Let me hear the grumbling of my fathers and uncles, blood
drop of my dead brother!

Still you say nothing.
So keep secret, secret. But
return to me, ever-returning.
And come inside, visitor, old rose, older than the remedy
    of the rose,
keeper of the back door, born
of sleep and the igneous kiss,
fed by what dies, rots, putrefies—
blood, pork-fat, and bone, fish-head,
shavings, peelings, curdled milk, what molds,
and stinks, this and the last and the last
year's leaves, mown grass, rotten apples, dead roses—
what I will not eat, but heap
on you in fall, each fall, that you may flourish,
ashen herald, that I may eat you, old
bitter rose.

8.

If with my mouth,
if with my clumsy tongue, my teeth,
if with my voice, my voice
of little girl, of man, of blood, and if

with blood, if with marrow, if with groin, lungs,
if with breath bristling with animal and vegetable, if with all
the beast in me, all the beauty,
I form one word,
then another, one
word
for every moment
which passes, and if I do so until
all words are spoken, then
begin again,
if I adore you, Rose,
with adoration become nonsense become
praise, could I stop our dying?
Could we sit together in new bodies, shoulder to tender shoulder,
the lovely and the thorned, the bitter and the failed,
the grave to the left of us, the sea to the right?
Could you rise and stand and bear
the weight of all the names I would give you?
Cup of Blood, Old Wrath, Heart O' Mine, Ancient of Days,
Whorl, World, Word.
O day, come!

     9.
You sag,
turn your face
from me, body
made of other bodies, each doomed.

Remember it was I who bled for you, I, born
hungry among the hungry,
third in the last generation of the old country,
of the family Plum, a brood
distinguished by madness,
tales of chains and wailing.

It was I who saw you withered and discarded,
I, who taught my father patience, and dulled the blade
   of his anger,
who eat you now, before morning,
when you must climb your ladder of thorns and grow to death.
I, middle stone in the row of stones
on my mother's ring, I,
the flawed stone, saw you dying
and revived you. I saw you
dying and called you mine.
I named you each day you remained:
Scorn, Banish, Grieve, Forgive, Love.


     10.

My meditation, my recitative,
I love you best this way,
an old brittle trumpet,
a shred of my mother's dress, no longer regal.
I love your nakedness.
Naked, shy flower, sweet
to my nose, and bitter
to my tongue, among
the dying things
are you and I.

## EATING TOGETHER

In the steamer is the trout
seasoned with slivers of ginger,
two sprigs of green onion, and sesame oil.
We shall eat it with rice for lunch,
brothers, sister, my mother who will
taste the sweetest meat of the head,
holding it between her fingers
deftly, the way my father did
weeks ago. Then he lay down
to sleep like a snow-covered road
winding through pines older than him,
without any travelers, and lonely for no one.

# I ASK MY MOTHER TO SING

She begins, and my grandmother joins her.
Mother and daughter sing like young girls.
If my father were alive, he would play
his accordian and sway like a boat.

I've never been in Peking, or the Summer Palace,
nor stood on the great Stone Boat to watch
the rain begin on Kuen Ming Lake, the picnickers
running away in the grass.

But I love to hear it sung;
how the waterlilies fill with rain until
they overturn, spilling water into water,
then rock back, and fill with more.

Both women have begun to cry.
But neither stops her song.

## ASH, SNOW, OR MOONLIGHT

Tonight two step out
onto a fourth story porch,
lean against the railing, and look at the moon.
Whether they intend to stay
a while, or only a moment because something awaits,
terrible or tender,
I can't say.
Whether one mutters to the other,
or they stand in silence,
I don't know. And I don't know
if they're here together in a brief repose,
or at the edge
of something incommunicable.
I don't know
if the man shivers now because he suddenly
sees the waste his life is to be in thirty years
on another shore, or because true autumn has begun
this moment of the present year, in a province
whose name evokes in half the world
a feeling of the vastness of the world.
I can tell you there is a war
going on, but don't ask me
to distinguish if it's ash, snow, or moonlight
that creases these people's faces.

Of this man, who each night hums a song and rocks his sons,
and falls asleep before they do, his tune long gone,
his labored breathing finally lulling them,
and this woman, who sweeps by rote or moonlight
the wood floor of their one room,
what news?

They won't stay long to gaze, for the night is cold.
They look neither young nor old,
though something about the way they
stand suggests fatigue.
They will die,
and one before the other to ensure grief.
But I don't know:
is it tenderness
or habit, perhaps a tender habit,
when the woman brushes her cheek
against the man's shoulder?
Do they admire the moon's ascent, or lament its decline?
How often have I seen these two?
Am I stricken by memory or forgetfulness?
Is this the first half of the century or the last?
Is this my father's life or mine?

# THE LIFE

My son grows limp
and heavy in my arms,
and I don't need to see his face
to know his eyes are closed,
his jaw hangs slack.
After hours of rocking, and pacing, and humming—
not a melody, but what
he likes, the single syllable his grandmother
has intoned to him since his birth, a monotone
nasal wail approaching mourning—
he's asleep, and I'm too tired
to get up from his chair, too dazed
to close my eyes, so keep
gaping out the window at the winter
sky, an hour ago black, now a deep blue,
and even as I think this, becoming
gray, the color changing
so fast, the light
coming so furiously that I think if I close my eyes and listen
I might hear grind
the great soft heart
of the sky. I close my eyes.
I listen.

I hear not the sky,
but the sea, or someone breathing near me,
and I watch
a boy ascend a ladder
into a ceiling of water, having slipped
out of his father's lap and arms, and replacing
his precise weight there

with an earthen jar,
having fooled his poor father,
whose sleep has finally come
after long bitterness, after hours
of hard thoughts about winter,
and money, and the exhaustions of fathers,
and the exhaustions of sons, and their loves
and trusts that shall be breached,
and all of our essential, human separateness.

It is a depthless hour of sweetest sleep
as the man's brow unwrinkles,
as if a hand had smoothed it,
the way a hand does a crushed
ball of paper, opens it,
smooths it, and smooths it,
so the poet might
begin again
his poem.

## THE WEEPERS

Were it not for the rain
beginning, big drops slapping
the gravestones, then spreading
like wounds, or smacking
the leaves overhead, first
one, then another, until
I stand beneath a chorus of mumbling
and leaves trembling—thus the rain
marks its passage through time, steadily
darkening what it touches,
and makes indistinguishable the moments
by narration in a monotonous voice—
were it not for the rain I'd stay.

I'd lean against this tree, and admire the beauty
of the weeping girls, the marble
twins who kneel together above a grave,
their white backs bent
in grief, their draped clothing conforming
here and there to the curve
of a breast, a hip, a thigh, while live
roses lie in their laps.

There have been times when I
was the one on the left,
hands folded between her knees,
withdrawn, almost inconsolable,
and times I was the other,
who embraces her sister, kisses her
on the round shoulder.
At any time, both
live in me
like sister branches of one tree,

the comforter and the comforted.
I am the father who comforts
his son, and I am the son
who returns in later years to give succor
to his father. I am the one
who walks among the dead,
and the one who waits
at home with warm bread and milk,
the way, I know, someone waits for me.

I recall an afternoon
we lay together, she
curled sideways and atop me, my body
cradling hers, which had been growing
round with our second son.
Lying that way,
her full hip fit
so perfectly
between my hip bones,
and with a gravity not unlike desire,
it conjured sadness
in my loins, almost pity.

O weepers, stone
girls weeping stone tears,
will you never recover?
Were it not for the rain, I'd linger
and maybe I'd weep.
But I'll do neither today, while someone
waits for me, and the rain
touches me, touches us
over and over, changes each of us,
shoulders and lips, roses and stones,
my love and the world,
all things which fit well.

## BRAIDING

### 1.

We two sit on our bed, you
between my legs, your back to me, your head
slightly bowed, that I may brush and braid
your hair. My father
did this for my mother,
just as I do for you. One hand
holds the hem of your hair, the other
works the brush. Both hands climb
as the strokes grow
longer, until I use not only my wrists,
but my arms, then my shoulders, my whole body
rocking in a rower's rhythm, a lover's
even time, as the tangles are undone,
and brush and bare hand run the thick,
fluent length of your hair, whose wintry scent
comes, a faint, human musk.

### 2.

Last night the room was so cold
I dreamed we were in Pittsburgh again, where winter
persisted and we fell asleep in the last seat
of the 71 Negley, dark mornings going to work.
How I wish we didn't hate those years
while we lived them.
Those were days of books,
days of silences stacked high
as the ceiling of that great, dim hall
where we studied. I remember
the thick, oak tabletops, how cool
they felt against my face
when I lay my head down and slept.

3.
How long your hair has grown.

Gradually, December.

4.
There will come a day
one of us will have to imagine this: you,
after your bath, crosslegged on the bed, sleepy, patient,
while I braid your hair.

5.
Here, what's made, these braids, unmakes
itself in time, and must be made
again, within and against
time. So I braid
your hair each day.
My fingers gather, measure hair,
hook, pull and twist hair and hair.
Deft, quick, they plait,
weave, articulate lock and lock, to make
and make these braids, which point
the direction of my going, of all our continuous going.
And though what's made does not abide,
my making is steadfast, and, besides, there is a making
of which this making-in-time is just a part,
a making which abides
beyond the hands which rise in the combing,
the hands which fall in the braiding,
trailing hair in each stage of its unbraiding.

6.
Love, how the hours accumulate. Uncountable.
The trees grow tall, some people walk away
and diminish forever.
The damp pewter days slip around without warning
and we cross over one year and one year.

## RAIN DIARY

It's not a host of heaven this morning
but my mother's voice
from another room
which wakens me.
A sweet tune she hums
to accompany the human task of making the bed
calls me back
to this body.
Mother, what did you dream?
Where were you last night
that even the storm didn't waken you?
Even as I came to your room, closed the windows,
and kissed you, you slept.

Night passed
with interminable rain.
Now, birds call
from the eaves again
in their thousand voices of China and Japan.
Where did the rain go? Across the fields? Out to sea?
Straight down
to my father
in his boat, with a lamp. Last night
I found the red book the world lost,
the one which contains the address of the rain,
all the names of the beloved dead, and how
and where they can be reached.
But shadows
fell across those pages
and a wind blew them away.
Where does the rain go? Where are my dead?

By now, my father's hair
has grown past his shoulders.
What name
would he answer to, this father
of sleepless nights and stories
of camps where his spit turned to blood?
Father of the thousand-mile-sadness, the rocking ship,
and the melancholy of trains.
Father of fatigue and
the bitter bowl,
whom I asked once, Where are we going?
My question could have been, In what country
will your pillow finally come to rest
and the rain call you home?
His answer would have been the same,
my father of this America and a divided tongue.
As a boy I lay quietly beside while he napped.
I was practicing to lie down
by his grave, father
beneath the grass
collecting the myriad waves of rain
in buckets and cans, the way we did
in Pittsburgh in 1964. I remember
his poverty, winters
and the trials by rain.
I remember holes in the ceiling,
his face leaning
into his own hands.
I remember my father of rain.

I looked for you in your shoes.
I found nothing
and the rain.
I tried your shirts, your pants,

called your sweaters mine,
but a dead man's things are
no one's, and this house screams out for you.
I searched the hours, perforated by rain.
I looked in the milk, the salt, cold water,
and found the rain.
I looked in the billowing curtains,
they were haunted with the rain.
Mother curled around it
and slept. She dreamed
she wandered, calling your name, and you
turned to her with no teeth.
She sought you in her cupped hands,
but nothing
followed the names of God,
and after *Amen*, the rain.

I want the rain
to follow me, to mark me
with a stripe down my chest and belly,
to darken my skin, and blacken my hair.
I want to be broken,
to be eaten by the anonymous mouths,
to be eroded like minutes and seconds,
to be reduced to water
and a little light.
I want to rise,
the doors of the rain to open,
I will enter, rain alive
among my fingers, embroidered on my tongue, and brilliant
   in my eyes,
I want to carry it in my shirt pocket,
devote my life to the discovery of its secret,
the one blessing it whispers.

Rain falls and does not
break. Neither does it stop,
but just pulls up
the gangplank and is gone.
It stands before me,
beside me, lies down
beneath me. How shall I praise it?
Rain knocks at my door and
I open. No one
is there, and the rain marching in place.

A rain has begun.
It is not the rain
that murmured all night at my window,
not the downpour I ran from in a field,
nor the storm which frightened me at sea.
It is moving toward me all my life.
Perhaps I shall know it.
Perhaps it is my father, arriving
on legs of rain, arriving,
this dream, the rain, my father.

## MY SLEEPING LOVED ONES

1.

This is no angel fallen in the noon,
but my sister asleep on the couch.
And don't mistake my stillness
for awe.
It's just that I don't want to waken her,
though I'd love to cup her chin in my palms,
bend down to her, like a mirror, and kiss her face.
But I'll do nothing,
just look a while, then leave
quietly. For this is noon,
time of rest, hour of tenderness
and the sleeping loved ones.

2.

The lovely comb
fashioned from bone
which I stole from
my mother's room
was laced with hair.
She'd been asleep,
afternoon came
like a question:
*What shall we do to play?*

3.

White labyrinth of summer.
Intense afternoon
approaches. It is my father's
nap-hour. Outside, one dove
tunnels the corridor of maples. The house

is quiet. The minutes
become a secret
I whisper with my brothers
in sun-bleached halls, rooms the dust
multiplies in.

No one sees his shirts go blind,
or knows his shoes are dying
of fatigue. No one
notices the population of shadows crowding his bed, or
    his favorite
white rose, breathless and sweating.
A black envelope arrives and cuts the hour in two: silence
and sobbing.

    4.
Today I drive from the grave,
my brothers asleep beside me.
The youngest rests his cheek
against his brother's shoulder,
his mouth slack and open, as if to whisper
*We are blessed.*
*We have entered the dominion of sleep.*

    5.
More than the cheekbones I inherited from my mother,
more than my left hand, the spear,
or my right hand, the hammer, more
than humility, like my father's heavy hand
on the back of my neck,
it is my love
for the sleeping ones
which recommends me.
It is my attention to their needs, my special tenderness
as I study this one's face,

or tuck a blanket around that one,
as I pull the shades down
so the sun isn't in their eyes,
or arrange flowers over their heads.
As I tip-toe by them
in absolute silence, and full of love,
observing their peace, yearning for a kiss, awaiting
their wakening.

## MNEMONIC

I was tired. So I lay down.
My lids grew heavy. So I slept.
Slender memory, stay with me.

I was cold once. So my father took off his blue sweater.
He wrapped me in it, and I never gave it back.
It is the sweater he wore to America,
this one, which I've grown into, whose sleeves are too long,
whose elbows have thinned, who outlives its rightful owner.
Flamboyant blue in daylight, poor blue by daylight,
it is black in the folds.

A serious man who devised complex systems of numbers and
    rhymes
to aid him in remembering, a man who forgot nothing, my father
would be ashamed of me.
Not because I'm forgetful,
but because there is no order
to my memory, a heap
of details, uncatalogued, illogical.
For instance:
God was lonely. So he made me.
My father loved me. So he spanked me.
It hurt him to do so. He did it daily.

The earth is flat. Those who fall off don't return.
The earth is round. All things reveal themselves to men only
    gradually.

I won't last. Memory is sweet.
Even when it's painful, memory is sweet.

Once, I was cold. So my father took off his blue sweater.

## BETWEEN SEASONS

Today I bring you cold chrysanthemums,
white as absence, long-stemmed as my grief.
I stand before your grave, a few unfallen
leaves overhead, the sucking mud beneath.

What survives best are chrysanthemums
in a month which arrives austere as grief.
The hearty blossoms persevere, unfallen.
Suffering even snow, they flourish beneath.

You walked in mornings among chrysanthemums,
and bowed to them as if to hear their grief.
Your sleeves grew damp from brushing unfallen
dew. A drop lay by your eye, and one beneath.

Truest to your nature were chrysanthemums,
brilliant while first snows descended like grief.
You watched them from your bed, your heart unfallen,
steadfast through winter, and then you slipped beneath.

What is it they told you, once, the chrysanthemums?
It made you sigh, *Ah, Grief!*
*Who savors you more than us, the unfallen,*
*long after we've forgotten the fallen beneath?*

## VISIONS AND INTERPRETATIONS

Because this graveyard is a hill,
I must climb up to see my dead,
stopping once midway to rest
beside this tree.

It was here, between the anticipation
of exhaustion, and exhaustion,
between vale and peak,
my father came down to me

and we climbed arm in arm to the top.
He cradled the bouquet I'd brought,
and I, a good son, never mentioned his grave,
erect like a door behind him.

And it was here, one summer day, I sat down
to read an old book. When I looked up
from the noon-lit page, I saw a vision
of a world about to come, and a world about to go.

Truth is, I've not seen my father
since he died, and, no, the dead
do not walk arm in arm with me.

If I carry flowers to them, I do so without their help,
the blossoms not always bright, torch-like,
but often heavy as sodden newspaper.

Truth is, I came here with my son one day,
and we rested against this tree,
and I fell asleep, and dreamed

a dream which, upon my boy waking me, I told.
Neither of us understood.
Then we went up.

Even this is not accurate.
Let me begin again:

Between two griefs, a tree.
Between my hands, white chrysanthemums, yellow
   chrysanthemums.

The old book I finished reading
I've since read again and again.

And what was far grows near,
and what is near grows more dear,

and all of my visions and interpretations
depend on what I see,

and between my eyes is always
the rain, the migrant rain.

## LI-YOUNG LEE

Li-Young Lee was born in 1957 in Jakarta, Indonesia, of Chinese parents. In 1959, his father, after spending a year as a political prisoner in President Sukarno's jails, fled Indonesia with his family. Between 1959 and 1964 they traveled in Hong Kong, Macau, and Japan, until arriving in America.

Li-Young Lee has studied at the University of Pittsburgh, University of Arizona, and SUNY Brockport. He lives in Chicago, Illinois, with his family and works as an artist for a fashion accessories company.